World Book Myths & Legends Series

ANCIENT GREEK MYTHS & LEGENDS

AS TOLD BY PHILIP ARDAGH

ILLUSTRATED BY VIRGINIA GRAY

World Book, Inc.
a Scott Fetzer company
Chicago

Myth or Legend?

Long before people could read or write, stories were passed on by word of mouth. Every time they were told, they changed a little, with a new character added here and a twist to the plot there. From these ever-changing tales, myths and legends were born.

What Is a Myth?

In early times, people developed stories to explain local customs and natural phenomena, including how the world and humanity developed. These myths were considered sacred and true. Most include superhuman beings with special powers. The ancient Greeks called these people heroes.

What Is a Legend?

A legend is very much like a myth. The difference is that a legend is often based on an event that really happened or a person who really existed in relatively recent times.

The ancient Greeks didn't separate genuine history from made-up stories about their past. The two have become so mixed up that it's very difficult to know what is fact and what is fiction.

Who Were the Ancient Greeks?

Greece lies between what is now Italy and Asia Minor. It is made up of a large peninsula—an area of land jutting out into the sea—and a scattering of islands. In about 2000 B.C. (that's almost 4,000 years ago), different wandering groups came to the Greek peninsula and settled with the people already living there.

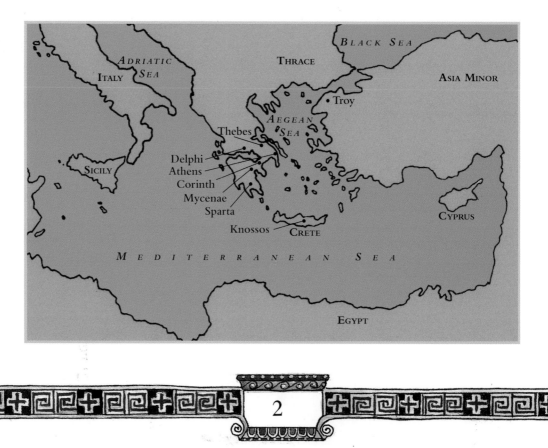

Over time, cities grew, people worshiped the same gods, and the Greeks became a powerful force in Europe. The ancient Greeks' empire and culture dominated Europe until the Romans took over Greece in 146 B.C.

GREEKS AND ROMANS

To many people, Roman mythology seems a copy of Greek mythology. For example, compare the Greek hero Heracles to the Roman hero Hercules. But in fact, many similarities can be traced to the Indo-European heritage shared by Rome and Greece.

HOW DO WE KNOW?

Greek myths and legends began to grow in the eighth century B.C., when the poems of a Greek poet named Homer became popular. The oldest surviving written works in Greek literature are two epic poems, called *The Iliad* and *The Odyssey*, both of which are said to have been written by him. They tell of the siege of the city of Troy and of the adventures of the hero Odysseus.

STATUES AND CARVINGS

Many characters in Greek myths and legends survive as statues and as carvings on ruined buildings. They also appear on pots. These are often painted in two styles: Attic black figures–black figures on a reddish-orange background; and Attic red figures–red figures on a black background. The illustrations in this book are loosely based on these ancient Greek styles.

The jar and vase above are painted in the Attic style and show scenes from Greek myths and legends. The central figure on the jar at the top is Dionysus, the Greek god of wine.

GODS, GODDESSES, & HEROES

There are many gods and goddesses in Greek myths, as well as heroes, kings, queens, monsters, and ordinary men and women. Greek gods and goddesses were immortal and could live forever. They were said to live on Mount Olympus, which is a real place in Greece. Here are some of the characters you will meet in this book. The names of similar Roman characters are shown in brackets.

ZEUS (Jupiter) King of the gods and god of thunder and lightning. Quick-tempered and often turns against humankind.

POSEIDON (Neptune) God of the sea. Uses his three-pronged spear, or trident, to make storms and control the waves.

HERA (Juno) Goddess wife of Zeus. Also quick to take offense.

HADES, sometimes called PLUTO (Dis) God of Tartarus, the Underworld of the dead, which is sometimes called the Kingdom of Hades.

HERACLES (Hercules) Hero son of Zeus, but not Hera. He had to complete twelve tasks, or labors, in his efforts to become one of the gods on Mount Olympus.

HERMES (Mercury) Messenger of the gods. Wears winged sandals.

DIONYSUS (Bacchus) God of wine. Carries a staff with vines wrapped around it.

PROMETHEUS Cleverest of the gods and a friend to humankind.

ATHENA (Minerva) Goddess of war. This terrifying warrior used her cunning to help the hero Perseus kill Medusa.

PERSEUS Hero whose most famous adventure was his quest to kill Medusa, the Gorgon.

APHRODITE (Venus) Goddess of love. Very beautiful and easily angered.

THESEUS Hero who faced the Minotaur –half bull, half beast–and freed its victims.

PANDORA The first woman. She was sent down to earth by the gods, and opened a jar that she'd been told to leave shut. Out of it poured all the evil and troubles of the world.

✛

BELLEROPHON Hero who rode through the skies on the back of the winged horse, Pegasus.

▣

PARIS Trojan hero who snatched Helen and took her to Troy.

✛

HELEN OF GREECE, later of TROY The most beautiful woman in the world. She was seized by Paris and taken to Troy. This is the event that led to the Trojan War.

▣

ODYSSEUS (Ulysses) Hero of Homer's *Odyssey* and many adventures.

✛

JASON Hero leader of the Argonauts. He had a ship called the *Argo*.

▣

OEDIPUS Tragic hero, doomed from birth. He killed his own father and married his mother.

✛

ORPHEUS Musician who followed his wife, Eurydice, to the Underworld of the dead to plead for her life.

The ancient Greeks carved images of the characters in their myths and legends on the walls of their buildings. At the Temple of Athena in Paestum (above), there are carved scenes of Greek heroes fighting in the Trojan War.

NOTE FROM THE AUTHOR
On the following pages you will find some of the most famous ancient Greek myths and legends. They can be read on their own or one after the other, like a story. Mostly they are fun and exciting, even though they can be gruesome or sad in places. I hope that you enjoy them and that this book will make you want to find out more about the lives of the ancient Greeks as well as their myths and legends.

MIDAS AND HIS GOLDEN TOUCH

The story of a man who fulfilled a prophecy and whose dream came true...but then became a dreadful curse.

Before King Midas was even a king of Phrygia–in fact, when he was still a little baby–he was left lying in the garden of his parents' palace. When it was time for his nursemaid to bring him out of the sun and into the cool of the palace, she let out a yelp of surprise.

There was a row of ants crawling up the baby prince, and each one was holding a golden grain of wheat. In turn each ant popped a golden grain into the baby's mouth and then made its way back down his body.

The nursemaid snatched up the young Midas, frantically brushed the remaining ants off him, and ran indoors to tell his parents what had happened. Rather than being upset as she'd expected, they were delighted at what she told them.

"This is a good omen!" said Midas' father. "I'm sure of it."

"We must go to the soothsayers to find out what it means," his mother agreed.

The soothsayers, who could see into the future, agreed with Midas' father. This was indeed a good sign. Golden wheat meant that real gold was to come. One day Midas would be a very rich man.

When Midas was old enough to understand, his parents told him of his future good fortune, but he soon forgot about it… until one day Dionysus, the god of wine, offered to grant him a wish.

Gods didn't usually grant humans wishes, but Midas had found in his garden Dionysus' friend, Silenus. He'd been left behind after one of the god's fantastic parties. Midas made sure that Silenus got back to Dionysus safely, which was why Midas was being offered a wish.

The king thought long and hard about what he wanted….

Suddenly he remembered the omen of the golden grains of wheat. "Let everything I touch turn to gold!" he said, with greedy excitement.

"Are you sure that's what you want?" grinned Dionysus, taking a gulp of wine and smacking his lips together with delight.

"Yes!" cried Midas, without a second thought.

"Then it is granted," said Dionysus. "Don't say I didn't warn you."

Midas bent down and picked up a twig. The moment his fingertips touched the wood, it turned to solid gold. Then he tried a leaf, a clump of grass,… an apple. Now he was enjoying himself! Hurrying back to his palace, he touched each marble column and they, too, turned to gold.

Midas sat down at the dinner table for a celebration feast, but it soon turned into a famine. When he reached out and touched a piece of bread, it turned to gold, and he couldn't bite into it. When the wine in his golden goblet reached his lips, it, too, turned to solid gold and couldn't be drunk.

Hungry and thirsty, Midas rose to his feet and paced up and down the marble floor in his golden sandals. Just then his young daughter ran into the room.

"Hello, daddy," she beamed, and before he could stop her, she threw her arms around him. The minute she touched her father, the king, she turned into a solid gold statue.

Midas hurried, weeping, to find Dionysus. "Please release me from this curse," he begged. "My greed got the better of me!"

"Very well," said the god of wine, with a chuckle. "There is a way to undo this magic," and he told the king what he had to do.

Following these instructions, Midas hurried to the source of the Pactolus River–the place where the water springs from the ground near Mount Tmolus–and washed himself.

Two things happened instantly: He was freed from the curse of his golden touch, and the sands on the bed of the Pactolus River turned a beautiful gold, which is why they are that color to this very day.

Medusa ~ the Snake-Haired Monster

With her hair of writhing serpents, just one glimpse of the terrifying Medusa could turn a person to stone.

Medusa was one of three monsters called the Gorgons. They had the bodies of women, snakes for hair, teeth like the tusks of wild boars, sharp claws, and wings of gold. Anyone who dared to look in the face of a Gorgon was turned to stone in horror.

The young hero Perseus was on a quest to kill Medusa. Fortunately he had the help of the gods. Athena, the goddess of war, went with him on his journey. Hermes, messenger of the gods, gave him a sharp knife to cut off Medusa's head. Some nymphs gave him a pair of winged sandals so that he could fly, a magic helmet to make him invisible, and a special pouch to keep Medusa's head in if he was successful.

One final gift was from Athena herself. She handed Perseus a shield.

"It contains no magic, but it is vital to your task," she explained.

"It's beautiful," said Perseus, admiring the gleaming shield. The bronze was so highly polished that he could see his face in it.

"Use it as a mirror," said the goddess, and the young hero understood.

Entering the place where the three Gorgons slept, Perseus squeezed through the silent crowd of stone victims. He knew that if he so much as glimpsed Medusa's face, he, too, would become a lifeless statue.

He turned his face to one side and held his shield in front of it, reflecting the sleeping Medusa in the shield's polished surface. Then, with his eyes fixed firmly on the shield, he made his way to her sleeping form. He pulled out the knife Hermes had given him and cut off Medusa's head without ever having to look at the hideous creature.

In this way the world was rid of one more terrifying monster, and Perseus earned his place among the heroes.

THE MAN WHO LOVED HIMSELF

The word *narcissistic* describes people who
spend a lot of time admiring how they look.
It comes from Narcissus, the name of
the main character–though hardly
a hero–of this legend.

There's no denying that Narcissus was very beautiful or handsome
or both. Many people came to him and declared their undying
love for him, but he treated them all in the same way–he rejected
them. He wanted nothing to do with them because he thought that
he was far too beautiful to be seen with them.

He decided that the person he would share his life with would
have to be *at least* as beautiful as he was, and in his opinion that
person would be very hard to find!

One day as Narcissus was walking through the forest, he felt
sure he was being followed.

"You show yourself!" he shouted.

"*You* show *yourself*!" a voice replied. The words were the same as his,
but Narcissus thought the voice was even more beautiful than his own.

"Come here," he pleaded. "Let me see you."

"Let *me* see *you*," the strange voice sighed.

Captivated by her voice and the fact that she–whoever she
was–thought and spoke in such a similar way to him, Narcissus
cried: "Let me hold you!"

"Let *me* hold *you*!" replied the voice, with obvious joy, and out of
the trees came a nymph called Echo.

She threw her arms around Narcissus, but when he saw that she was
nothing more than an ordinary nymph, he pushed her roughly away.

"I could never love you!" Narcissus screamed, with a cruel smile.

"Love you," said Echo with great sadness. She longed to tell
Narcissus just how much she loved him, but was unable to speak of her
feelings. In the past, Echo had upset Zeus with all her talking, so he
punished her by taking her own speech away. All she could do was
repeat what had just been said.

Rejected by Narcissus like all others before her, Echo left the forest
with great sadness, but she still loved him.

Time passed, and one day Narcissus came to a clear, pure spring
filling a pool at Donacon in Thespia. He sat on the grassy bank and
looked into the water. There he saw a perfect reflection of himself
in all his beauty…and promptly fell in love with it.

When he realized that the most beautiful person he had ever
seen was himself, he decided that life wasn't worth living anymore.
He pulled out his dagger and, with a final cry of "goodbye," plunged
it straight into his heart.

"Goodbye," sobbed Echo, who still so loved Narcissus that she had
followed him and was hiding nearby.

Where Narcissus' blood touched the ground, a single white flower
sprouted from the earth, which is named narcissus after him. But unlike
the man, the flower is not aware of its own beauty.

THE MINOTAUR IN THE MAZE

King Asterion of Crete had no children of his own, so he adopted three brothers. When he died, one of the brothers, Minos, seized power. This was just the beginning of a tale that would lead to death, destruction, and despair.

Minos said that he'd offer a prayer to the gods to try to prove to everyone that he was the rightful ruler of Crete. He claimed that if the gods answered his prayer, this would prove beyond any doubt that they were happy for him to be king.

"What shall I pray for?" he asked a crowd outside the palace.

"Pray that a great white bull comes charging out of the sea!" someone shouted, saying the first unlikely thing that came into his head.

"And if this prayer is answered," demanded Minos, "am I then your rightful king?"

A cry of "Yes!" rang out through the crowd, and Minos was overwhelmed with joy.

Now Poseidon is the god of the sea, so if Minos wanted a great white bull to come charging out of it, he'd have to pray to Poseidon. But how could he tempt Poseidon into answering his prayer?

King Minos was a very crafty person. He knew that there was nothing the gods liked more than an animal sacrifice. In this ceremony an animal was killed in a god's name and offered up to one of them. The more spectacular the animal, the greater the honor to the god. Minos would pray to Poseidon for the bull and promise to sacrifice it to him afterward.

So Minos built an altar to the god of the sea and prayed for a sacrificial bull to come charging out of the waves....

13

And so it did. The pure white beast burst to the surface and swam to the shore. When the crowds saw this, they could see that the gods were on Minos' side and that he must surely be their rightful ruler.

But there was still the matter of sacrificing the bull. It was the most impressive bull Minos had ever seen. He couldn't bring himself to kill this marvelous animal, so he broke the promise he had made to Poseidon in his prayer. He sent for one of the bulls from his herd and sacrificed that instead.

Poseidon felt cheated. In revenge he made Pasiphaë, Minos' wife and queen, fall in love with the bull, and there was nothing she could do about it.

Minos was delighted when Pasiphaë said she was going to have a baby, but the delight soon turned to horror when the child was born— it was half human and half bull. Minos wasn't the father—the bull was. Horrified and ashamed at the disgrace he had brought on his family by betraying Poseidon, King Minos hurried to an oracle—a kind of soothsayer—to ask what he should do.

"How can I avoid the scandal and dishonor?" he asked.

"Ask the craftsman Daedalus to build you a palace at Knossos," replied the oracle. "Hide your shame with cunning."

King Minos took his advice and asked the famous inventor and designer Daedalus to build a palace with the most complicated maze underneath. He called this maze the Labyrinth.

The Labyrinth was a place of endless corridors and winding passages, with many a dead end and only one true path to and from the center. At its very heart King Minos hid Pasiphaë and the monster with the man's body and bull's head—away from the prying eyes of the people of Crete. Pasiphaë named her grotesque son Asterius, but as he grew up, he became known as the Minotaur.

Now King Minos once had a much-loved son called Androgeus, but he had been killed by the Athenians—people from Athens—who were ruled by King Aegeus.

To make up for his son's death, Minos was sent seven young men and seven young women from Athens as a tribute every nine years.

The tribute came to the island of Crete in a ship rigged with a black sail. The young men and women were led into the winding passages of the Labyrinth. It was impossible for them to find their way out. There were too many twists and turns in the dark, shadowy tunnels. Alone and frightened, all they could do was to wait for the Minotaur to catch the smell of human flesh in the air....

When he reached them, the echoes of their cries rang through the Labyrinth.

When it was time for the Athenians to send their third tribute, 18 years after the first, Theseus, King Aegeus' own son, offered to be one of the seven men to go. His father was horrified.

"Don't worry," Theseus tried to reassure him. "We will keep your promise and send King Minos his tribute, but I also promise that all 14 of us shall return home safely."

"Then take this white sail with you, my brave son," said King Aegeus. "If the ship returns without you, let the black sail remain rigged to the mast. If you succeed in your task, rig this white one. Then I will know of your victory and safe return before you even reach our shores."

"It's a white sail you shall see," his son assured him.

Once the tribute had been chosen, Theseus secretly let two of the young women go and replaced them with two boys. King Aegeus would keep his promise–the Minotaur would indeed be sent 14 Athenians, but not all would be as it seemed....

When Theseus and the tribute arrived on the shores of Crete, King Minos was there to greet them. At his side stood his daughter, Ariadne. No sooner had she laid eyes on Theseus than she fell in love with him. When her father turned his attention elsewhere, Ariadne whispered to Theseus, "I will help you kill the Minotaur."

"But how will I find my way in the Labyrinth?" Theseus whispered.

"I know a way," said Ariadne, "and I will show you if you promise to take me back to Athens and marry me."

"I promise," said Theseus, mouthing the words in silence as King Minos turned back to him.

"Tonight you are my prisoners," said the king. "Tomorrow you meet the Minotaur. Now come."

That night Ariadne met secretly with Theseus and handed him a magic ball of thread. "This was given to me by Daedalus," she explained. "It was he who built the maze beneath the palace. Tie the loose end of the thread to the door post as you enter the Labyrinth, and then drop the ball on the floor. It will lead you to the Minotaur."

"And there I will kill it!" hissed Theseus.

Ariadne nodded. "Once this is done, pick up the ball, rolling up the thread as you go, and it will lead you back to the entrance."

Armed only with a sword given to him by Ariadne, Theseus entered the Labyrinth alone that night. As Ariadne had instructed, he tied one end of the thread to the door post, then dropped the ball to the floor. Like any ball of thread, it began to unravel, but—*unlike* any other—it made its way along the passages that led toward the center of the maze… and to the Minotaur.

Meanwhile, under the cover of darkness, the Athenian men overpowered the guards outside their room. The women were having equal success. The two boys who had disguised themselves as women took their guards completely by surprise, killing them quickly and quietly. Now all they could do was wait.

While the others waited, Theseus made his way along the twisting tunnel, barely able to see the ball of thread unrolling silently at his feet. The flickering light from the flaming torches gave the Labyrinth a strange orange glow, and there was a smell of death in the air. Then suddenly the ball came to a standstill, and Theseus became aware of the heavy breathing of an animal. The Minotaur was asleep!

Theseus raised his sword, just as the Minotaur opened one eye.

The creature leaped up to face him. With one swift motion, Theseus slashed off the Minotaur's head, then followed the thread back to the entrance. While it was still dark, he joined the others. Ariadne guided them back to their ship and they slipped out of the harbor.

No one knows for sure the reason why, but despite everything Ariadne had done for him, Theseus broke his promise to her. When they stopped for a few days at the island of Dia, later called Naxos, he left her there, sleeping, and traveled home without her.

No one can say for certain, either, why Theseus forgot to take down the black sail and rig the white one. Perhaps he was so pleased with his success. . . or perhaps he was saddened at having betrayed Ariadne. Whatever the reason, the black sail remained fluttering on the rigging of the ship as it pulled into the harbor.

Watching from the clifftops, his father, King Aegeus, saw that the sail was not the white one. He took this to mean that his son had died in his attempt to kill the Minotaur. With a cry of despair, he jumped from the cliffs and drowned in the sea that is now called the Aegean in memory of him.

PROMETHEUS' GIFT TO HUMANS

According to some myths, it was the god Prometheus who created the human race. It's no wonder, then, that he wanted it to thrive.

One day when an argument arose over which part of an animal should be sacrificed to the gods and which part should be kept by humans, Zeus called in Prometheus to judge. Knowing that Zeus always thought "bigger is better," Prometheus took a dead ox and separated the meat from the bone and fat. Next he squeezed the meat inside a small parcel, and the bones and fat together inside a much larger one. He took the two parcels to Zeus.

"You choose," Prometheus said to the king of the gods, and just as he'd guessed, Zeus chose the bigger parcel…. And that is how it came to be that humans eat the meat, while the less pleasant fat and bones are offered up to the gods.

Zeus found out he'd been tricked and was furious. "Humans may keep the meat," he bellowed, "but I'll not give them fire to cook it!"

Prometheus thought that this was most unfair. He secretly went up to Mount Olympus and lit a torch from the flames of the fiery chariot of Helios, the sun god. Quickly he snapped a piece of glowing wood from the torch and hid it in the middle of a vegetable called fennel. Then he slipped away and came down to earth where he shared the secret of fire with our ancestors.

When Zeus learned what had happened, he had Prometheus chained, naked, to a pillar in the Caucasus Mountains. There, every day and all day, a vicious, hungry eagle tore at his liver until it was eaten. Every night the liver would grow again, ready for the following day's torture. There Prometheus remained until he was rescued by Heracles, the greatest hero of them all.

ICARUS ~ THE BOY WHO REACHED TOO HIGH

Daedalus was one of the greatest inventors of his day, but he could not control his jealous rage, or the recklessness of his son Icarus.

Daedalus lived in Athens and was famous for his clever inventions. People came from far and wide for his advice and ideas on how to make things. He had a young nephew, called Talos, who helped him with his work. Very soon Talos became a better inventor than Daedalus, and people began to ask him for advice instead of asking Daedalus.

Daedalus put a stop to this once and for all when, in a fit of jealousy, he pushed Talos from the roof of the temple of Athena. With Talos dead, Daedalus left Athens in a hurry–which was how he came to settle on the island of Crete.

Unfortunately for Daedalus, he fell out with King Minos after Theseus killed the Minotaur. The angry king threw the inventor into the Labyrinth along with his son Icarus.

With help they escaped from their prison, but how could they escape from the island? It wouldn't be long before they were tracked down and locked up again. Daedalus soon came up with a plan. He trapped birds and used their feathers to build two huge pairs of wings. He sewed the feathers onto cotton and sealed them in place with wax. He then strapped one pair of wings to his son and the other to himself.

"If we jump off that high ground together, Icarus, and you do as I do, we'll escape from this island with our lives," said the old man, "but there are a few simple rules we must follow."

"Yes, yes," said Icarus, impatiently. He was anxious to leave before anyone discovered them.

"Listen!" said his father. "You mustn't fly too high or too low. Simply follow me and do as I do."

Then, after a silent prayer to the gods, Daedalus launched himself off the ground and soared through the air. The wings worked! They really worked! He was flying!

Soon father and son had left the island of Crete behind them, but it was not long before Icarus forgot his father's words of warning.

This was such fun! A cool breeze blew from the sea below. The sun warmed them from above. The sky was a beautiful clear blue. The farther they flew, the more carefree and careless Icarus became.

He soared, he swooped, he dived through the air and then flew up and up and up, until he was far too close to the sun. The heat of the sun's rays melted the wax that held the feathers in place. The wings began to fall apart....

"Father!" cried Icarus. "Father! Help me!"

But Daedalus was too far ahead to hear his son's cries. It was only when the inventor heard a loud splash in the calm waters below that he realized what had happened. Icarus had hurtled to his death in the waters near the island of Samos.

Daedalus had been punished by the gods for pushing his nephew, Talos, from the temple roof. As he flew to safety, his tears fell from the skies and into the sea, where his son Icarus had met his tragic fate.

PEGASUS ~ THE WINGED HORSE

When Perseus cut off the head of the terrifying Medusa, a winged horse leapt from her dead body. This was Pegasus, a beautiful and brave creature.

Night after night Bellerophon dreamed of the wonderful winged horse that he'd seen drinking at the spring at Peirene. Every morning he'd wake up and wish that this beautiful steed could be his. One night the dream changed. The goddess Athena appeared to him and handed him a golden bridle.

"With this, Pegasus shall be yours," she told him.

So the horse had a name: Pegasus. Bellerophon woke with the word on his lips. In his hands he felt something cold, and he looked down to see that he really was clutching a golden bridle. This had been no ordinary dream.

Bellerophon hurried back to Peirene and there–sure enough–Pegasus came in to land. He crept forward and slipped the magic bridle onto the horse. Pegasus' eyes met his, and each understood the other.

The hero and the winged horse had many adventures together. For a while Bellerophon lived in the palace of King Proitos of Argos. Unfortunately the queen fell in love with him, but he felt nothing for her. Hurt by his rejection, she went to her husband, King Proitos, and claimed that it was Bellerophon who was in love with her.

Saddened by the news, the king sent the unsuspecting Bellerophon to deliver a message to King Iobates of Lycia. The message was sealed shut, and it requested that Iobates kill the one who brought it.

When the king read the message, he didn't want blood on his hands. He decided that the best way to kill Bellerophon was to send him on an impossible quest. His kingdom was plagued by the Chimaera, a fire-breathing monster, with a lion's head, a goat's body, and a serpent's tail.

"You must kill it for me, Bellerophon," he said, fully expecting him to become the Chimaera's next victim.

But Bellerophon was cunning as well as brave. Riding on the back of Pegasus, he swooped down on the beast and thrust a spear deep into its throat. The end of the spear was made of lead, which melted in the heat of the monster's fiery breath. The molten lead then poured down the Chimaera's throat, burning its insides and killing it.

King Iobates was so pleased at being rid of the Chimaera that he chose to ignore King Proitos' request. He not only let Bellerophon live, he also let him marry his daughter and have half of his kingdom.

Over time Bellerophon became more and more self-important. He thought that he was the greatest hero of all time and was very conceited. One day he decided that he was equal to the gods and would fly on Pegasus to Mount Olympus to claim his rightful place there.

Zeus would have none of it. He sent a single gadfly to bite Pegasus. The winged horse reared up in surprise, throwing its rider from its back. Bellerophon fell to earth with a bump and spent the rest of his days as a poor outcast.

Today Pegasus lives with the gods on Mount Olympus, carrying Zeus' thunderbolts on its back.

THE TWELVE LABORS OF HERACLES

There are many heroes in the myths and legends of ancient Greece, but none is more popular than Heracles.

Heracles was the son of Zeus and a woman called Alcmene, whom Zeus had tricked into loving him. Zeus' wife, the goddess Hera, hated Heracles from the start. She sent two giant, venomous serpents to kill Heracles when he was just a baby....But Heracles was no ordinary child. The following morning Alcmene found her son happily cooing in his cot, holding the two dead snakes that he'd strangled with his bare hands—saving not only his own life, but that of his half brother, too.

Heracles grew into a handsome man of incredible strength. He could fight well with all types of weapons, but his favorite was a club that he had cut and shaped from an olive tree.

Zeus had originally planned that Heracles would become king of Mycenae, but because she had been so badly betrayed, Hera had made sure that the honor went to Heracles' cousin, Eurystheus.

She did agree that if Heracles could succeed at twelve special tasks set by King Eurystheus, then he would be entitled to become one of the immortal gods of Mount Olympus.

These tasks were the twelve labors of Heracles. Each was designed to be impossible, for Hera didn't want Heracles to succeed.

The first labor was to kill the Nemean lion—a lion whose skin was so thick that no weapon could pierce it. Heracles tried with his sword and his club, but each attempt failed. In the end he wrestled with the mighty beast and strangled it, as he had the serpents as a baby.

Heracles returned to King Eurystheus. He wore the lion's skin to prove that he'd been successful. He'd found that the only way he could skin the lion was by using one of its own claws as a knife.

Eurystheus was amazed and a little frightened to see Heracles. He'd expected news of Heracles' death to reach him, not Heracles himself!

"And what is my second labor, cousin?" asked Heracles, beaming.

"To kill the Hydra," said Eurystheus, trying to hide a triumphant grin. Surely even the great Heracles wouldn't survive this challenge?

The Hydra was a many-headed monster that lived in the swamplands of Lerna. The creature was said to be immortal, as each time anyone struck off one of its heads, two more grew in its place. The goddess Hera made this labor even harder for Heracles by sending an enormous crab to lurk in the swamp and nip at his legs.

But Heracles had a plan. Every time he cut off one of the Hydra's heads, his cousin, Iolas, touched a flaming torch to the stump of the neck. This stopped the blood from flowing and new heads from growing. Finally, with the last head chopped off and the last stump scorched, the Hydra lay dead.

Now that Heracles had proved successful at killing beasts, Eurystheus gave him a labor that required the hero to bring one back alive.

He was sent to capture the Ceryneian Hind—a deer of great grace and beauty with golden antlers. The deer could run at great speed, and it took Heracles a year before he caught it in Arcadia. This was a sacred animal, so rather than tying it up or harming it, Heracles pleaded with the goddess Artemis to command the creature to go with him to the king. Artemis agreed… so Heracles was successful, and Eurystheus had to set him a fourth, near-impossible task.

There was a wild boar destroying crops and farm animals around Mount Erymanthos. It was a fierce animal, and the local people were more than a little frightened of it. It had become known as the Erymanthian Boar, and Heracles' fourth labor was to capture it. This he managed to do by cornering the boar in a snowdrift and binding it with rope. He then carried it back to King Eurystheus on his shoulders.

Heracles marched into the palace with the boar held high. It is said that when the king saw the beast with its huge tusks, he was so frightened that he scuttled off his throne and hid in a large brass jar!

Then came the fifth labor. All Heracles had to do was to clean out the Augean Stables. This sounds simple enough, but Heracles had one day to do it, and the stables had never been cleaned. They were piled high with horse manure and cattle dung.

Heracles completed this task in an ingenious way. Using his superhuman strength, he dug trenches that diverted the water from two nearby rivers and washed the stables clean!

On the shores of Lake Stymphalos was a flock of the most dreadful birds you can imagine. They had razor-sharp beaks and claws and wings of metal. They not only hunted and ate the animals that stopped to drink at the lake, but they also ate humans. Heracles' sixth task was to rid the world of them all.

When Heracles arrived, he found that he could kill the odd one or two Stymphalian Birds when they were in flight. An arrow fired from his bow could pierce their underbellies. The trouble was that most of the flock were roosting in the trees, and no shouting or clapping would make them leave the safety of the branches.

Fortunately for Heracles, not all the goddesses were on Hera's side. The goddess Athena, a daughter of Zeus, gave Heracles a special bronze rattle to help him in his task.

The rattle proved very useful. Every time Heracles shook it under the trees, the birds took flight, and Heracles could shoot them down. In this way he completed his sixth labor.

Next Heracles had to capture the Cretan Bull. This was the same bull that Poseidon had given to King Minos for him to sacrifice, but which the king had kept for himself. This huge white bull was now on the loose in Crete, killing any islanders who crossed its path. But it was no match for Heracles. He brought it back to Eurystheus, who wanted to offer it as a sacrifice to Hera.

But because her enemy Heracles had caught it, the goddess wanted nothing to do with the bull.

This brings us to the eighth labor of Heracles—to capture the flesh-eating horses of the terrible King Diomedes of Thrace. Heracles killed the evil king, and while the Horses of Diomedes were busy feeding off their own master, Heracles herded them together and drove them to Mycenae. One thing we can be certain of—Eurystheus must have been horrified when he saw them.

Heracles was proving to be so successful at his tasks that when Eurystheus' daughter said that she longed to own the Girdle of the Amazon, the king decided to see if Heracles could bring it back as his next labor. The girdle was a piece of bronze armor, worn by Hippolyta, queen of the mighty race of warrior women. Whether he had to kill her for it, or whether she willingly gave it to him as one warrior to another, isn't really clear, but—yet again—Heracles returned triumphant.

This left just three labors. The tenth was to bring the Cattle of Geryon back to Mycenae. Geryon wasn't a place—it was a giant, and no ordinary giant at that. It had three heads, six arms, and a weapon in each hand—but still Heracles defeated it and managed to herd the cattle to Eurystheus.

Heracles' eleventh task was to collect the Golden Apples of the Hesperides. On his journey he found the chained Prometheus suffering endless attacks from the eagle, as his punishment from Zeus. Heracles killed the bird, set Prometheus free, then went on his way.

Only gods or goddesses were allowed into the garden of Hesperides where the apples grew, so Heracles had to ask Atlas to go in for him. It was Atlas' job to hold up the heavens, so Heracles had to hold the heavens while Atlas picked the apples.

"I'll take the apples to the king for you," said Atlas on his return. "I'm tired of holding up the heavens, and you can do it just as well as I."

"That's fine," said Heracles, thinking quickly.

"Before you go, would you hold the heavens again, for just a moment, while I make a pad for a sore spot on my shoulders? If I'm taking over your task, I need to be as comfortable as possible."

Atlas put down the apples and held up the skies once more.

"Thank you," Heracles grinned. He snatched up the apples and was off on his way, leaving the tricked Atlas fuming with rage.

This left Heracles one last task. If he could succeed in this twelfth labor, then he would have earned the right to become a god. This time he had to enter the Underworld itself. He was to bring the king the dog that guarded the entrance to Tartarus. Cerberus was no ordinary dog. It had three dogs' heads, a mane of writhing snakes, and a serpent's tail, but even this monster could do nothing against Heracles' brute strength.

When Eurystheus came face to face with the dog from the Underworld, he was almost speechless.

"T–T–T–Take i–i–i–it b–b–b–back," he spluttered, running from the room in horror.

Heracles had successfully completed the last of his twelve labors. No one could deny his right to become a god and to take his place on Mount Olympus.

ODYSSEUS AND THE ONE-EYED GIANT

**A hero of many adventures, Odysseus had
to use quick wit, strength, and cunning
to defeat Polyphemus the Cyclops.**

Odysseus was returning home from the Trojan War when he visited the island of the Cyclopes. These were terrifying giants with a single eye in the center of their foreheads. They tended sheep, which they ate whole.

Odysseus and some of his men entered a cave and rested and sheltered there. It was the home of a Cyclops called Polyphemus, who was one of the sons of the sea god, Poseidon. When evening came, the one-eyed giant returned with his flock. With his sheep safe inside, the huge and hideous creature rolled an enormous stone across the mouth of the cave. It was so big and so heavy that no human—no *team* of humans—could hope to move it. Odysseus and his men were trapped.

Catching sight of the frightened humans, Polyphemus the Cyclops snatched up two of Odysseus' crew and swallowed them whole. The next morning he ate another two, then rolled back the stone to let his sheep out. He couldn't believe his luck—he had a pantry full of humans!

"What is your name, little man?" asked the giant, as he stepped out of the cave and began to roll the rock back across the opening. "Are you one of these heroes I hear so much about?"

"Me, a hero?" laughed Odysseus. "I am a nobody." Then an idea began to form in his mind. "In fact, my name is Nobody."

"Greetings, Nobody. I look forward to eating you on my return," grinned the Cyclops, as the giant boulder blocked out the sun.

That night Polyphemus returned with his sheep and—as Odysseus watched helplessly—snatched up another two men and ate them. Then the Cyclops drank some wine and fell into a deep sleep.

Odysseus didn't waste any time. He pulled out a huge wooden stake, which he'd hidden out of sight in the shadows, heated the point in the fire, then climbed onto the sleeping giant's chest. With all his might he thrust the stake into Polyphemus' single eye. The giant screamed, loud enough to bring the other Cyclopes to the outside of his cave.

"Are you all right, Polyphemus?" cried one, through the rock across the entrance. He didn't want to roll it aside in case Polyphemus was simply having nightmares–he wouldn't be too pleased if all his sheep escaped for no reason!

"Are you under attack?" asked another Cyclops, aware that strangers had been seen on the island.

Remembering the name that Odysseus had told him, Polyphemus shouted out, "Nobody's hurting me!"

Misunderstanding Polyphemus' cries, and satisfied that he was in no danger, the other Cyclopes returned to their parts of the island.

"Nobody's hurting me!" the Cyclops cried, expecting help to arrive.

The next morning, blinded but not defeated, Polyphemus felt his way along the stone walls of his cave. He rolled the huge rock just far enough for a single sheep to pass through.

"I'll let my sheep out to graze one at a time, Nobody," he declared. "But you and your men will remain here until I decide to eat you. I don't need to see to eat–just a hearty appetite and sharp teeth."

As each sheep passed through the gap in the cave opening, Polyphemus stroked its fleece to check that it really was a sheep and not a human trying to slip past him.

Imagine his surprise, therefore, when he heard Odysseus' voice outside his cave.

"You should have thought to feel underneath the sheep," he bellowed. "We strapped ourselves beneath their bellies."

Just to make absolutely sure that the Cyclops knew who had outwitted him, he added, "And I am certainly not a nobody. My name is Odysseus. Remember it well!"

ORPHEUS AND THE UNDERWORLD

**The story of a man's music that brought tears
to the eyes of the dead and gave a beautiful
nymph a second chance to live.**

Orpheus played the lyre so beautifully that the birds in the air,
the fish in the water, and the animals above and below ground
would come to listen to his music.

This wonderful gift made him very happy, but his wife, the nymph
Eurydice, made him happier still.

Try to imagine then his utter horror when Eurydice stepped on
a poisonous snake, which bit her foot. The poison quickly took effect,
and Orpheus could see her life draining away from her.

Orpheus followed his wife down to Tartarus–the world of the dead
ruled over by Hades and his queen, Persephone. He pleaded with them
to let his wife live again and played them some sad music. So powerful
was this music that it made the dead forget their woes and cry for him.

"Your music speaks to me," said Hades. "Its sadness tells of a true
love, so I release Eurydice to you. Go now, and she will follow, but
don't look at her until you reach the surface, or she will be lost to you."

Bursting with joy and declarations of thanks, Orpheus dashed up
to the world of mortals, hearing Eurydice's footsteps behind him.

When he could see daylight ahead he wanted to sing for joy!
"We're nearly there," he said, turning to her. He had forgotten Hades'
command, and Eurydice fell back into the Underworld never to be
seen again.

Orpheus spent his days in the forest, but all the tunes he played
were sad ones. Those who looked after him soon became jealous of
his undying love for the dead nymph, and they decided to kill him.
His grave is said to be easy to find because a nightingale hovers over
it, forever singing to his memory.

THE WOODEN HORSE OF TROY

The exciting thing about a surprise gift is that you never know what might be inside. That can also be the danger.

According to Greek legend the war between the Greeks and the people of Troy was a long and bloody one, and at the center were Helen, the most beautiful woman in all of Greece, and Paris, the Trojan prince who loved her.

Paris was the son of the king and queen of Troy. When he was born, his mother dreamed that she was giving birth to a flaming torch. Fearful that this was a bad omen, King Priam ordered that the child be left on a hillside to die.

Luckily Paris was found by a group of shepherds who brought him up. He led a remote life, away from the influence of others, and this is why he was called upon by the goddesses Hera, Athena, and Aphrodite to settle an argument about which of them was the prettiest.

Each goddess tried to bribe Paris to choose her. Hera promised him power, while Athena offered him the skills to make him a fine warrior. But it was Aphrodite's bribe that he couldn't resist. She said that if he chose her as the prettiest, Paris would win the love of the world's most beautiful woman, Helen of Greece. So Paris declared Aphrodite the winner, instantly making enemies of the other two goddesses.

Paris went to Sparta, convinced that Helen would fall in love with him. He snatched Helen from her husband and took her back to Troy.

A huge fleet of Greek heroes set sail for Troy to try to bring her back. When words failed, they laid siege to the city.

After nine long years of war, someone in the Greek ranks hatched a plan and built a huge, hollow, wooden horse on wheels. Some say it was the hero Odysseus' idea. Others say that it was Epeius' master plan.

One morning the sentries at the gates of Troy woke to find the extraordinary horse left outside. The next thing they noticed was that the Greek armies had gone. Reports soon reached Troy that the Greek fleet had been seen sailing away. The war was over!

A captured Greek soldier claimed that the horse had been built as an offering to the goddess Athena so that she might give them the wind for their sails.

Helen, who, as Aphrodite had promised, now loved Paris with all her heart, was suspicious of the wooden horse, but none of the Trojans would listen to her. They wanted to bring this offering to Athena inside the walls of the city.

That night, while the city slept, the Greek fleet came silently back to the shore, and the armies made their way to the walls of Troy. Inside the city there was a movement from within the horse. It was full of Greek soldiers, who had been hiding there all the time!

They opened a trap door in the horse's belly, lowered a rope ladder, and climbed down under the cover of darkness. Overpowering the sentries, they opened the gates and let in their comrades.

There were some dreadful deeds done that night, ending with the city of Troy being burned to the ground. The dream of Paris' mother that he was a flaming torch had indeed been a terrible omen.

JASON AND THE ARGONAUTS

Jason, heir to the throne of Iolcus, had come to claim his crown. First he had to fetch the Golden Fleece from a magical ram—a task intended to destroy him. Aboard his ship, the *Argo*, Jason and his crew had many adventures.

"Good luck, Jason!" shouted a voice in the small crowd that had gathered on the shore to see Jason off on his quest. The *Argo* floated proudly on the dawn waves, its brilliant white sail glowing orange in the light of the rising sun.

On its crowded decks stood Jason and his 49-strong crew, the Argonauts. Never before had such a brave and heroic crew sailed together in one vessel. It included everyone from Heracles the hero, to Atalanta the huntress. Jason raised his hand in salute to the crowd.

Many had expected Heracles to captain the *Argo*, but he insisted that Jason should be in charge of the ship as well as the quest for the Golden Fleece at Colchis.

Their first stop was at the island of Lemnos, where Jason and the Argonauts were greeted by fierce, helmeted warriors shaking spears. When Jason managed to convince them that his mission was a peaceful one, the warriors removed their helmets. They revealed themselves to be beautiful women dressed in their dead husbands' armor.

Jason soon discovered that Lemnos was inhabited entirely by women. They had murdered all the men—except for one who was set adrift in a boat without oars—because the men had treated them badly.

The Lemnian women were very welcoming and eager for the Argonauts to stay and marry them. It was a long time—some say a year—before Jason's crew managed to return to their ship.

Soon the Argonauts were hurtled into further adventures....

They were forced to leave Heracles behind at a place called Arcton. Heracles and another Argonaut had gone in search of a third who had been lured to an underwater grotto by love-sick nymphs. A good wind had come up, and Jason was forced to set sail without them.

In Thrace the Argonauts visited King Phineus, who had been blinded by the gods for being too good at seeing into the future. Despite his blindness Phineus still had the gift of soothsaying, and Jason wanted to ask his advice about what lay ahead for him and his crew of Argonauts.

"I will tell you what you need to know," replied Phineus, his sightless eyes staring ahead into nothingness. "But first you must rid me of the curse of the Harpies."

"What are they?" asked Jason.

The blind man smiled. "You shall soon see," he said. "Dine with me."

Soon a vast banquet was laid out before Jason and his ship's company. Just as King Phineus reached for a piece of bread, the air in the hall was filled with the sound of beating wings and screams of hideous laughter.

Jason looked up and was shocked to see two terrifying winged women swoop down and snatch food from Phineus' table. Again they swooped, then yet again, snatching up the food.

"These are the Harpies," sighed Phineus, "and I am dying of hunger because they will not let a morsel of food pass my lips."

Jason called across the table to the Argonauts Calais and Zetes.

"Help Phineus so that he might help us," he cried.

The two Argonauts nodded, bade their friends farewell, then flexed their wings–for they were sons of Boreas, the North Wind–and flew up after the Harpies, chasing them from the palace.

With the Harpies gone Phineus was free to eat and drink at last. When he'd had his fill, he kept his promise to Jason. Phineas told him things that might help him on his journey, including how to deal with the Symplegades Rocks at the entrance to the Bosphorus Strait.

Finally the Argonauts said goodbye to the soothsayer king and climbed back aboard the *Argo*.

With the wind behind them, Jason and his remaining Argonauts finally reached the Symplegades Rocks. They loomed out of the sea mists before them like a pair of sentinels. Between the two rocks was a narrow passage of water that they would have to row down.

Unlike many an unwary seafarer who had gone before them, Jason's crew had the advantage of Phineus' knowledge. He had warned them that these rocks moved. They smashed together, crushing any unsuspecting thing that passed between them.

"Release the dove," Jason instructed, following Phineus' plan.

As the bird flew between the rocks, the Argonauts watched carefully to see how quickly they came together to try to crush the creature. They watched the path the dove took and the speed with which it flew. It had just completed the journey, when the rocks crashed together, catching a few of its tail feathers.

"We must row as fast as the dove flew," Jason announced. "Any slower and we'll lose more than our tail feathers!"

So the sail was lowered, and the Argonauts took their places at the oars. They rowed between the Symplegades Rocks at a speed no one has rowed before or since. Even then they only just made it. There was a splintering of wood, as the very tip of the stern of the *Argo* was crushed and torn away, and the rest of the ship passed safely through.

Now it was on to Colchis, where King Aeëtes held the Golden Fleece. Here the gods—who so often like to meddle in the affairs of humans—decided that it would be good sport to make the king's daughter, Medea, fall in love with Jason.

On hearing of Jason's quest, Medea's father agreed to let him have the fleece, so long as he fulfilled some near-impossible feats.

"Firstly, you must hitch my two fire-breathing bulls to a plow," he commanded. "And then you must plow the great Field of Ares for me."

"That is a huge field, your majesty," said Jason. "It will take days."

"You have only one," said the king. "And that is not all. You must sow dragons' teeth in the freshly tilled soil, and face the consequences."

The other Argonauts gasped. No single person could complete such a difficult task, and who knew what might grow from dragons' teeth?

"And if I succeed, the Golden Fleece is mine?" asked Jason, staring into the face of King Aeëtes.

"You have my word," the king nodded, knowing in his heart that the fleece was safe, for the man who stood before him was bound to fail.

What he hadn't bargained for was that his own daughter, Medea, would help Jason. Hopelessly in love with him, she gave Jason a special ointment that would protect him from the bulls' fiery breath and from any weapons he might encounter—but for only a day.

Jason smeared the magic ointment all over himself, then faced the bulls and yoked them to the plow. Although the ointment protected him from harm, he used his own brute strength and determination to harness the beasts and to plow the Field of Ares in a day.

Night fell, and it was time for Jason to sow the dragons' teeth. No sooner had the last handful fallen into the rich, tilled soil, than they grew into hundreds upon hundreds of armed soldiers.

As quick as a flash, Jason used an old trick. He snatched up a stone and threw it at the back of the head of one of the soldiers. The dazed soldier spun around and began to fight the man behind him. Soon the squabble spread, and the soldiers were fighting one another rather than turning their attention to Jason. Swords were drawn, spears were thrown, and after much bloody in-fighting, every man lay dead.

Jason had accepted the king's challenge and—with a little help from Medea—he had been victorious. The Golden Fleece was rightfully his, but Aeëtes had no intention of keeping his word.

Unaware of her love for Jason, the king told his daughter that he planned to kill Jason and the Argonauts. Medea hurried to Jason and led him to a sacred grove where the Golden Fleece hung from a tree.

This precious prize was guarded by a famous dragon of a thousand coils—a dragon that could not be killed.

"That terrible beast is bigger than my ship!" gasped Jason. "How can I hope to get past it to the fleece?"

"Dragons are relatives of the snake, and all snakes can be charmed," said Medea, and she began to sing a strange and wonderful song, with magical and soothing words.

As the dragon's eyelids began to droop, Medea stepped forward slowly and sprinkled sleeping dust into its eyes. No sooner were the dragon's eyes completely shut than Jason dashed forward and pulled the Golden Fleece from the branch.

Safely back on the *Argo* with Medea and his Argonauts, Jason set sail to claim the throne of Iolcus. Even then his adventures were not over. It took more of Medea's trickery to help him win the crown….

Though Jason had many more adventures, his death was not a hero's death. He betrayed Medea, and at the end of his life, he was sad and lonely. Sitting by the now-old *Argo*, remembering past glories, he was struck on the head and killed by a timber from the ship that had carried him into legend.

OEDIPUS ~ DOOMED BY PROPHECY

The gods can be cruel at times, and they certainly were to Oedipus. Even before he was born, he was condemned to be a murderer, and worse....

According to myth, when Pandora opened a jar and let disease and despair into this world, she also released Hope, the one thing that makes the lives of mortals bearable when times are hard. But there was no hope for Oedipus. Even before he was born, Apollo prophesied that he would grow up to kill his own father.

When Oedipus' father, King Laius of Thebes, heard this, he panicked. "We must kill the baby as soon as it is born," he said.

"No!" cried Queen Jocasta. "He will still be our son, and to kill him would be to go against the prophecy of the gods! Who knows what troubles we might bring down upon the whole kingdom of Thebes!"

"Then we must send him away," said the king. "If he perishes, that is the will of the gods...." He smiled to himself. He would make *sure* that the baby perished, even if he didn't actually kill him.

"And if he survives?" sobbed Jocasta.

"If he survives, he'll have no idea who his father is, and the prophecy may yet fail!" said the king.

When the baby was born, Jocasta just had time to give him his first kiss before he was snatched by his father, the king. Laius strode from her bed chamber and–out of sight of his sobbing wife–tied up the bawling infant and nailed his feet together with a spike.

"Take him to Mount Cithaeron," he ordered a servant, "and leave him there to die."

Too frightened to go against the word of his arrogant master, the servant did as he was told. There is no way of knowing what thoughts were in his mind as he carried out this dreadful deed.

Perhaps it was by chance that he left the child near a flock of sheep. Perhaps it was the will of the gods that a shepherd discovered the baby. He was a poor but kind man, who tended the boy's wounds and named him Oedipus, which means "swollen foot." He took the child to the palace at Corinth, knowing that King Polybus and Queen Periboea were kind people and didn't have any children of their own.

King Polybus and his queen treated the child with love and kindness, and Oedipus grew into a fine prince, but not a happy one. As a young man he looked nothing like the king and queen–whom he thought of as his mother and father–and he felt very out of place.

He decided that he should go to an oracle at Delphi, who was famous throughout Greece for her advice and wisdom, and see whether she could explain his strange feelings.

"What makes me stand out from others?" he asked.

"Go!" said the oracle.

"No," insisted Oedipus. "I must know."

The message the oracle gave him was a shattering one.

"You will kill your father and marry your mother!" she boomed.

Thinking that Polybus and Periboea were his father and mother, Oedipus was horrified. They were such loving parents! He swore never to return to Corinth and never to see them again. That way they would be safe from him.

With great sadness Oedipus began to travel aimlessly from land to land. One day he was walking down the road, his scarred feet aching, when a horse reared up in front of him.

"Out of my way, you lowly scum!" a voice bellowed. The horse was pulling a chariot carrying an angry, red-faced man. "Out of my way!"

Until that moment Oedipus had had every intention of stepping aside to let the chariot pass, but something in the man's voice made him stand his ground. There was no need for such rudeness.

When Oedipus refused to move, the man in the chariot cried out with an uncontrollable rage and tried to run him down.

Oedipus managed to leap aside, safe from the thundering hoofs and crushing wheels. He lunged at the man, who toppled off the back of his chariot and became entangled in his horse's reins. The last sight Oedipus had of the man was of him being dragged behind the chariot in a cloud of dust.

What Oedipus had no way of knowing was that this was King Laius, his true father. The first part of the prophecy had come true.

Shaken by the man's rage and horrific death, Oedipus went on his way. He arrived in the outskirts of Thebes to find it in turmoil. A large Sphinx—half lion, half woman, with eagle's wings—had taken up position at the entrance to the city. Everyone who tried to pass her was presented with a riddle.

If the passersby could answer it, they were free to pass into Thebes. If they failed, the Sphinx killed and ate them. The riddle remained unchanged because, so far, no one had been able to answer it correctly. The number of dead was rising, and fear had spread throughout the city.

Oedipus knew nothing of this, so he was shocked to be confronted by the strange beast. "Answer me this riddle," she demanded. "What walks on four legs in the morning, two legs at midday, and three legs at night?"

Oedipus thought long and hard. Whereas other people had been frightened, and quick to give any answer in the hope it was the right one, Oedipus took his time.

"By morning, you could mean the early years," said Oedipus slowly, looking into the frightening eyes of the Sphinx for clues as to whether he had the right idea. Her eyes were expressionless.

"By midday, you could mean the middle years," he continued.

"What is your answer?" snapped the creature.

"And by evening, you could mean the last years of life," said Oedipus.

"Your answer?" the Sphinx screeched.

"A human," said Oedipus. "In his childhood, he crawls on all fours. As an adult he stands upright and walks on two legs, but as he gets older, he needs a walking stick to help him."

"Yes! Yes! Yes!" wailed the Sphinx, the words turning into a mournful cry as she flew up Mount Phicium and hurled herself–wings unopened–to the valley below, smashing herself to death on the rocks.

Freed from the curse of the Sphinx, and learning of the death of the hated King Laius, the people of Thebes made Oedipus their king in grateful thanks. His wisdom had saved them from the monster.

To seal the authority of his kingship, Oedipus then wed Laius' widowed queen, Jocasta, unaware that he was fulfilling the prophecy of the oracle at Delphi. He was now married to his own mother.

Neither knowing the other's true identity, the new king and queen of Thebes were very happy and, over time, had four children. Then a terrible plague came to the land. People died, crops failed, and the water turned sour. It was almost as though Thebes and its people were being punished by the gods.

Oedipus returned to the oracle at Delphi to seek advice. "How can I rid my kingdom of this terrible plague?" he asked.

"By casting out the murderer of Laius," replied the oracle.

When Oedipus returned to Thebes, he declared that whoever had murdered King Laius should be sent into exile, unaware that he was the murderer!

The truth was finally revealed when blind Teiresias, the most famous soothsayer in all of Greece, had an audience with Queen Jocasta.

"You have news of how to save our people?" she asked.

"I have news that may well save the people of Thebes, but it is not news that will please you, your majesty," said Teiresias.

"You speak in riddles," said the queen. "If you can help us stop this awful plague, please tell me what you know."

"It was Oedipus who killed your husband, Laius," said the soothsayer.

"You lie!" screamed Jocasta, leaping to her feet. "The prophecy said that our own son would kill him, and Oedipus is the son of Polybus and Periboea of Corinth." She sent a messenger to Corinth to be sure.

"No. He's not our child," Queen Periboea told Jocasta's messenger.

"Oedipus was brought to us by a shepherd, his tiny feet spiked together and bleeding, but we brought him up as our own son. We have never known who his real parents were."

On hearing this news Queen Jocasta summoned the servants and found the one who had taken her baby son to the mountainside all those years ago, on the orders of King Laius.

His head bowed in shame, the servant spoke of the baby boy. "His hands were tied, and his tiny feet were spiked together," he confirmed.

Jocasta thought of Oedipus' feet and their distinctive scars. Teiresias, the blind soothsayer, was right–Oedipus really *was* her son, and she was married to him!

Horrified and shamed, Queen Jocasta hanged herself. Oedipus was filled with such a mixture of hopelessness and rage that he blinded himself, realizing that it had been impossible to escape the prophecy. He spent the rest of his life as a wandering beggar.

The sadness of this tale is that Oedipus was doomed from birth. He was lucky in one thing, though. However sad he was, and wherever he traveled thereafter, his daughter Antigone went with him, because she truly loved her father.

Myths and Legends Resources

Here is just a sampling of other resources to look for. These resources on myths and legends are broken down into groups. Enjoy!

General Mythology

The Children's Dictionary of Mythology *edited by David Leeming* (Franklin Watts, 1999). This volume is a dictionary of terms, names, and places in the mythology of various cultures around the world.

Creation Read-aloud Stories from Many Lands *retold by Ann Pilling* (Candlewick Press, 1997). This is a collection of sixteen stories retold in an easy style and presented in three general groups: beginnings, warmth and light, and animals.

The Crystal Pool: Myths and Legends of the World *by Geraldine McCaughrean* (Margaret K. McElderry Books, 1998). Twenty-eight myths and legends from around the world comprise this book. They include the Chinese legend "The Alchemist" and the Celtic legend "Culloch and the Big Pig."

Encyclopedia Mythica
http://www.pantheon.org/areas/mythology/
From this page of the *Encyclopedia Mythica* site you can select from any of five countries to have the mythology of that area displayed.

A Family Treasury of Myths from Around the World *retold by Viviane Koenig* (Abrams, 1998). This collection of ten stories includes myths from Egypt, Africa, Greece, and other places around the world.

Goddesses, Heroes and Shamans: The Young People's Guide to World Mythology *edited by Cynthia O'Neill and others* (Kingfisher, 1994). This book introduces the reader to over five hundred mythological characters from around the world.

Gods, Goddesses and Monsters: An Encyclopedia of World Mythology *retold by Sheila Keenan* (Scholastic, 2000). This beautifully illustrated book discusses the characters and themes of the myths of peoples from Asia to Africa, to North and South America.

The Golden Hoard: Myths and Legends of the World *retold by Geraldine McCaughrean* (Margaret K. McElderry Books, 1995). This book contains twenty-two myths and legends that are exciting, adventurous, magical, and poetic.

The Illustrated Book of Myths: Tales and Legends of the World *retold by Neil Philips* (Dorling Kindersley, 1995). This beautifully illustrated collection brings together many of the most popular of the Greek and Roman, Norse, Celtic, Egyptian, Native American, African, and Indian myths.

Kids Zone: Myths and Fables from Around the World
http://www.afroam.org/children/myths/myths.html
Just click on your choice of the sixteen stories listed, and it will appear in full text.

Legends http://www.planetozkids.com/oban/legends.htm
From this Web page you can get the full text of any of the many listings.

Mythical Birds and Beasts from Many Lands *retold by Margaret Mayo* (Dutton, 1996). This book is a collection of stories that illustrate the special powers of birds and beasts that have become a part of folklore around the world.

Mythology *by Neil Philip* (Alfred A. Knopf, 1999). This superbly illustrated volume from the "Eyewitness Books" series surveys the treatment of such topics as gods and goddesses, the heavens, creation, the elements, and evil as expressed in various mythologies around the world.

Mythology *CD-ROM for Mac and Windows* (Thomas S. Klise, 1996). Educational games and puzzles, a glossary, and a testing section are all part of this CD introduction to Greek and Roman mythology.

Myths and Legends *by Neil Philip* (DK Publishing, 1999). More than fifty myths and legends from around the world are explained through works of art, text, and annotation by one of the world's foremost experts on mythology and folklore.

The New York Public Library Amazing Mythology: A Book of Answers for Kids *by Brendan January* (John Wiley, 2000). Over two hundred questions and answers introduce myths from many ancient cultures, including Egyptian, Greek, Roman, Celtic, Norse, and Native American.

Plays from Mythology: Grades 4-6 *by L.E. McCullough* (Smith and Kraus, 1998). Twelve original plays are included, each with suggestions for staging and costumes.

Sources for Mythology
http://www.best.com/~atta/mythsrcs.html
In addition to defining mythology and distinguishing it from legend and folklore, this Web site lists primary sources for myths from many regions of the world, as well as magazines, dictionaries, and other resources relating to mythology.

Sun, Moon and Stars *retold by Mary Hoffman* (Dutton, 1998). More than twenty myths and legends from around the world, all explaining what was seen in the sky, make up this exquisitely illustrated book.

AFRICAN

African Gods and their Associates
http://www3.sympatico.ca/untangle/africang.html
This Web page gives you a list of the African gods with links to further information about them.

African Myths
http://www.cybercomm.net/~grandpa/africanmyths.html
Full text of several tales from the Kenya, Hausa, Ashanti, and Nyanja tribes are included in this Web site.

Anansi and the Talking Melon *retold by Eric A. Kimmel* (Holiday House, 1994). Anansi, a legendary character from Africa, tricks Elephant and some other animals into thinking that the melon in which he is hiding can talk.

Children's Stories from Africa *4 Video recordings (VHS)* (Monterey Home Video, 1997). Among the African Legends on this page: "How the Hare Got His Long Legs," "How the Porcupine Got His Quills," "The Brave Sititunga," and "The Greedy Spider."

The Hero with an African Face: Mythic Wisdom of Traditional Africa *by Clyde W. Ford* (Bantam, 2000). "The Hero with an African Face" is only one of the several stories included in this book, which also includes a map of the peoples and myths of Africa and a pronunciation guide for African words.

Kings, Gods and Spirits from African Mythology
retold by Jan Knappert (Peter Bedrick Books, 1993). This illustrated collection contains myths and legends of the peoples of Africa.

Legends of Africa *by Mwizenge Tembo* (Metro Books, 1996). This indexed and illustrated volume is from the "Myths of the World" series.

Myths and Legends *retold by O. B. Duane* (Brockhampton Press, 1998). Duane has vividly retold some of the most gripping African tales.

CELTIC

Celtic Myths *retold by Sam McBratney* (Peter Bedrick, 1997). This collection of fifteen illustrated stories draws from English, Irish, Scottish, and Welsh folklore.

Excalibur *retold by Hudson Talbott* (Books of Wonder, 1996). In this illustrated story from the legends of King Arthur, Arthur receives his magical sword, Excalibur

Irish Fairy Tales and Legends *retold by Una Leavy* (Robert Rinehart, 1996). Cuchulainn, Deirdre, and Fionn Mac Cumhail are only three of the legendary characters you will meet in this volume.

Irish Myths and Legends
http://www.mc.maricopa.edu/users/shoemaker/
  Celtic/index.html
This Web site is for those more serious in their study of Irish myths and legends.

King Arthur *by Rosalind Kerven* (DK Publishing, 1998). This book from the "Eyewitness Classic" series is a retelling of the boy who was fated to be the "Once and Future King" It includes illustrated notes to explain the historical background of the story.

Robin Hood and His Merry Men *retold by Jane Louise* Curry (Margaret K. McElderry, 1994). This collection contains seven short stories of the legendary hero Robin Hood, who lived with his band of followers in Sherwood Forest.

The World of King Arthur and his Court: People, Places, Legend and Love *by Kevin Crossley-Holland* (Dutton, 1998). The author combines legend, anecdote, fact, and speculation to help answer some of the questions regarding King Arthur and his chivalrous world.

CHINESE

Asian Mythology *by Rachel Storm* (Lorenz, 2000). Included in this volume are myths and legends of China.

Chinese Culture
http://chineseculture.about.com/culture/
  chineseculture/msub82.htm
Use this Web page as a starting point for further exploration about Chinese myths and legends.

Chinese Mythology by *Anne Birrell* (Johns Hopkins, 1999). This comprehensive introduction to Chinese mythology will meet the needs of the more serious and the general reader

Chinese Myths and Legends *retold by O. B. Duane and others* (Brockhampton Press, 1998). Introductory notes by the author give further explanation of the thirty-eight stories included in this illustrated volume.

Dragons and Demons by *Stewart Ross* (Cooper Beech, 1998). Included in this collection of myths and legends from Asia are the Chinese myths "Chang Lung the Dragon" and "The Ugly Scholar."

Dragons, Gods and Spirits from Chinese Mythology *retold by Tao Tao Liu Sanders* (Peter Bedrick Books, 1994). The stories in this book include ancient myths about nature, the gods, and creation as well as religious legends.

Fa Mulan: The Story of a Woman Warrior *retold by Robert D. San Souci* (Hyperion, 1998). Artists Jean and Mou-Sien Tseng illustrate this Chinese legend of a young heroine who is courageous, selfless, and wise.

Land of the Dragon: Chinese Myth by *Tony Allan* (Time-Life, 1999). This volume from the "Myth and Mankind" series includes many of China's myths as well as examination of the myth and its historical roots.

Selected Chinese Myths and Fantasies
http://www.chinavista.com/experience/story/story.html
From this Web site and its links you will find several Chinese myths that are enjoyed by children as well as the history of Chinese mythology.

EGYPTIAN

Egyptian Gods and Goddesses by *Henry Barker* (Grosset and Dunlap, 1999). In this book designed for the young reader, religious beliefs of ancient Egypt are discussed, as well as their gods and goddesses.

Egyptian Mythology A-Z: A Young Reader's Companion by *Pat Remler* (Facts on File, 2000). Alphabetically arranged, this resource defines words relating to Egyptian mythology.

Egyptian Myths *retold by Jacqueline Morley* (Peter Bedrick Books, 1999). Legends of the pharaohs, myths about creation, and the search for the secret of all knowledge, make up this illustrated book.

The Gods and Goddesses of Ancient Egypt by *Leonard Everett Fisher* (Holiday House, 1997). This artist/writer describes thirteen of the most important Egyptian gods.

Gods and Myths of Ancient Egypt by *Mary Barnett* (Regency House, 1996). Beautiful color photographs are used to further explain the text in this summary of Egyptian mythology.

Gods and Pharaohs from Egyptian Mythology *retold by Geraldine Harris* (Peter Bedrick Books, 1992). The author gives some background information about the Ancient Egyptians and then retells more than twenty of their myths.

Myth Man's Egyptian Homework Help
http://egyptmyth.com/
Cool Facts and Fun for Kids and *Egyptian Myth Encyclopedia* are only two of the many wonderful links this page will lead you to.

Myths and Civilizations of the Ancient Egyptians by *Sarah Quie* (Peter Bedrick Books, 1998). The author intersperses Egypt's myths with a history of its civilization in this illustrated volume.

The Secret Name of Ra *retold by Anne Rowe* (Rigby Interactive Library, 1996). In this Egyptian myth, Isis tricks Ra into revealing his secret name so that she and her husband Osiris can become rulers of the earth.

Tales from Ancient Egypt *retold by George Hart* (Hoopoe Books, 1994). The seven tales in this collection include stories of animals, of Isis and Horus, of a sailor lost on a magic island, and of pharaohs and their magicians.

Who's Who in Egyptian Mythology by *Anthony S. Mercatante* (Scarecrow Press, 1995). The author has compiled a concise, easy-to-use dictionary of ancient Egyptian deities.

GREEK

Allta and the Queen: A Tale of Ancient Greece by *Priscilla Galloway* (Annick Press, 1995). This made-up story, which is based on Homer's epic poem, *The Odyssey*, reads like a novel.

Cupid and Psyche *retold by M. Charlotte Craft* (Morrow Junior Books, 1996). This classic love story from Greek mythology will appeal to young and old.

Gods and Goddesses by *John Malam* (Peter Bedrick Books, 1999). This volume is packed with information about the important gods and goddesses of ancient Greece, including Zeus, Hera, Athena, and Hades.

Greek and Roman Mythology by *Dan Nardo* (Lucent, 1998). The author examines the historical development of Greco-Roman mythology, its heroes, and its influence on the history of Western civilization.

Guide for Using D'Aulaires' Book of Greek Myths in the Classroom *by Cynthia Ross* (Teacher Created Materials, 1993). This reproducible book includes sample plans, author information, vocabulary-building ideas, cross-curricular activities, quizzes, and many ideas for extending this classic work.

Hercules *by Robert Burleigh* (Harcourt Brace, 1999). Watercolor and color pencil illustrations help to tell the story of Hercules's final labor in which he went back to the underworld and brought back the three-headed dog, Cerberus.

Medusa *by Deborah Nourse Lattimire* (Joanna Cotler Books, 2000). The author/illustrator of this book re-creates the tragedy of one of the best-known Greek myths, the tale of the beautiful Medussa whose conceit causes a curse be placed on her.

The Myths and Legends of Ancient Greece *CD-ROM for Mac and Windows* (Clearvue, 1996). This CD conveys the heroic ideals and spirit of Greek mythology as it follows ten of the best-known myths.

Mythweb http://www.mythweb.com/ This Web page provides links to Greek gods, heroes, an encyclopedia of mythology, and teacher resources.

Pegasus, the Flying Horse *retold by Jane Yolen* (Dutton, 1998). This Greek myth tells of how Bellerophon, with the help of Athena, tames the winged horse Pegasus and conquers the monstrous Chimaera.

The Race of the Golden Apples *retold by Claire Martin* (Dial, 1991). Caldecott Medal winners Leo and Diane Dillon have illustrated this myth of Atalanta, the beautiful Greek princess.

The Random House Book of Greek Myths *by Joan D. Vinge* (Random House, 1999). The author retells some of the famous Greek myths about gods, goddesses, humans, heroes, and monsters, explaining the background of the tales and why these tales have survived.

The Robber Baby: Stories from the Greek Myths *retold by Anne Rockwell* (Greenwillow Books, 1994). Anne Rockwell, a well-known name in children's literature, has put together a superbly retold collection of myths that will be enjoyed by readers of all ages.

NORSE

Beowulf *by Welwyn Wilton Katz* (Groundwood, 2000). The illustrations in this classic legend are based on the art of the Vikings.

Favorite Norse Myths *retold by Mary Pope Osborne* (Scholastic, 1996). These fourteen tales of Norse gods, goddesses, and giants are based on the oldest written sources of Norse mythology, *Prose Edda* and *Poetic Edda*.

The Giant King *by Rosalind Kerven* (NTC Publishing Group, 1998). Photos of artifacts from the Viking Age illustrate these two stories that are rooted in Norse mythology.

Gods and Heroes from Viking Mythology *by Brian Branston* (Peter Bedrick Books, 1994). This illustrated volume tells the stories of Thor, Balder, King Gylfi, and other Nordic gods and goddesses

Handbook of Norse Mythology *by John Lindow* (Ambcc, 2001). For the advanced reader, this handbook covers the tales, their literary and oral sources, includes an A-to-Z of the key mythological figures, concepts and events, and so much more.

Kids Domain Fact File http://www.kidsdomain.co.uk/teachers/resources/ fact_file_viking_gods_and_goddesses.html This child-centered Web page is a dictionary of Viking gods and goddesses.

Myths and Civilization of the Vikings *by Hazel Martell* (Peter Bedrick, 1998). Each of the nine stories in this book is followed by a non-fiction spread with information about Viking society.

Norse Mythology: The Myths and Legends of the Nordic Gods *retold by Arthur Cotterell* (Lorenz Books, 2000). This encyclopedia of the Nordic peoples' myths and legends is generously illustrated with fine art paintings of the classic stories.

Odins' Family: Myths of the Vikings *retold by Neil Philip* (Orchard Books, 1996). This collection of stories of Odin, the All-father, and the other Viking gods Thor, Tyr, Frigg, and Loer is full of excitement that encompasses both tragedy and comedy.

Stolen Thunder: A Norse Myth *retold by Shirley Climo* (Houghton Mifflin, 1994). This story, beautifully illustrated by Alexander Koshkin, retells the Norse myth about the god of Thunder and the recovery of his magic hammer Mjolnir, from the Frost Giany, Thrym.

NORTH AMERICAN

Buffalo Dance: A Blackfoot Legend *retold by Nancy Can Laan* (Little, Brown and Company, 1993). This illustrated version of the Native North American legend tells of the ritual performed before the buffalo hunt.

The Favorite Uncle Remus *by Joel Chandler Harris* (Houghton Mifflin, 1948). This classic work of literature is a collection of stories about Brer Rabbit, Brer Fox, Brer Tarrypin, and others that were told to the author as he grew up in the South.

Iktomi Loses his Eyes: A Plains Indian Story *retold by Paul Goble* (Orchard Books, 1999). The legendary character Iktomi finds himself in a predicament after losing his eyes when he misuses a magical trick.

The Legend of John Henry *retold by Terry Small* (Doubleday, 1994). This African American legendary character, a steel driver on the railroad, pits his strength and speed against the new steam engine hammer that is putting men out of jobs.

The Legend of the White Buffalo Woman *retold by Paul Goble* (National Geographic Society, 1998). This Native American Plains legend tells the story of the White Buffalo Woman who gave her people the Sacred Calf Pipe so that people would pray and commune with the Great Spirit.

Myths and Legends for American Indian Youth http://www.kstrom.net/isk/stories/myths.html Stories from Native Americans across the United States are included in these pages.

Snail Girl Brings Water: a Navajo Story *retold by Geri Keams* (Rising Moon, 1998). This retelling of a traditional Navajo re-creation myth explains how water came to earth.

The Woman Who Fell from the Sky: The Iroquois Story of Creation *retold by John Bierhirst* (William Morrow, 1993). This myth describes how the creation of the world was begun by a woman who fell down to earth from the sky country, and how it was finished by her two sons.

SOUTH AMERICAN (INCLUDING CENTRAL AMERICAN)

Gods and Goddesses of the Ancient Maya *by Leonard Everett Fisher* (Holiday House, 1999). With text and illustration inspired by the art, glyphs, and sculpture of the ancient Maya, this artist and author describes twelve of the most important Maya gods.

How Music Came to the World: An Ancient Mexican Myth *retold by Hal Ober* (Houghton Mifflin, 1994). This illustrated book, which includes author notes and a pronunciation guide, is an Aztec pourquoi story that explains how music came to the world.

Llama and the Great Flood *retold by Ellen Alexander* (Thomas Y. Crowell, 1989). In this illustrated retelling of the Peruvian myth about the Great Flood, a llama warns his master of the coming destruction and leads him and his family to refuge on a high peak in the Andes.

The Legend of the Poinsettia *retold by Tomie dePaola* (G. P. Putnam's Sons,1994). This beautifully illustrated Mexican legend tells of how the poinsettia came to be when a young girl offered her gift to the Christ child.

Lost Realms of Gold: South American Myth *edited by Tony Allan* (Time-Life Books, 2000). This volume, which captures the South American mythmakers' fascination with magic, includes the tale of the first Inca who built the city of Cuzco, as well as the story of the sky people who discovered the rain forest.

People of Corn: A Mayan Story *retold by Mary-Joan Gerson* (Little, Brown, 1995). In this richly illustrated creation story, the gods first try and fail, then try and fail again before they finally succeed.

Tales from the Rain Forest: Myths and Legends from the Amazonian Indians of Brazil *retold by Mercedes Dorson* (Ecco Press, 1997). Ten stories from this region include "The Origin of Rain" and "How the Stars Came to Be."

WHO'S WHO IN MYTHS AND LEGENDS

This is a cumulative listing of some important characters found in all eight volumes of the **World Book Myths and Legends** series.

A

Aegir (EE jihr), also called Hler, was the god of the sea and the husband of Ran in Norse myths. He was lord of the undersea world where drowned sailors spent their days.

Amma (ahm mah) was the creator of the world in the myths of the Dogon people of Africa. Mother Earth was his wife, and Water and Light were his children. Amma also created the people of the world.

Amun (AH muhn), later Amun-Ra, became the king of gods in later Egyptian myths. Still later he was seen as another form of Ra.

Anubis (uh NOO bihs) in ancient Egypt was the god of the dead and helper to Osiris. He had the head of a jackal.

Ao (ow) was a giant turtle in a Chinese myth. He saved the life of Kui.

Aphrodite (af ruh DY tee) in ancient Greece was the goddess of love. She was known for her beauty. The Romans called her Venus.

Arianrod (air YAN rohd) in Welsh legends was the mother of the hero Llew.

Arthur (AHR thur) in ancient Britain was the king of the Britons. He probably was a real person who ruled long before the age of knights in armor. His queen was Guinevere.

Athena (uh THEE nuh) in ancient Greece was the goddess of war. The Romans called her Minerva.

Atum (AH tuhm) was the creator god of ancient Egypt and the father of Shu and Tefnut. He later became Ra-Atum.

B

Babe (bayb) in North American myths was the big blue ox owned by Paul Bunyan.

Balder (BAWL dur) was the god of light in Norse myths. He was the most handsome of all gods and was Frigga's favorite son.

Balor (BAL awr) was an ancient chieftain in Celtic myths who had an evil eye. He fought Lug, the High King of Ireland.

Ban Hu (bahn hoo) was the dog god in a myth that tells how the Year of the Dog in the Chinese calendar got its name.

Bastet (BAS teht), sometimes Bast (bast) in ancient Egypt was the mother goddess. She was often shown as a cat. Bastet was the daughter of Ra and the sister of Hathor and Sekhmet.

Bellerophon (buh LEHR uh fahn) in ancient Greek myths was a hero who captured and rode the winged horse, Pegasus.

Blodeuwedd was the wife of Llew in Welsh legends. She was made of flowers woven together by magic.

Botoque (boh toh kay) in Kayapó myths was the boy who first ate cooked meat and told people about fire.

Brer Rabbit (brair RAB iht) was a clever trickster rabbit in North American myths.

C

Chameleon (kuh MEEL yuhn) in a Yoruba myth of Africa was a messenger sent to trick the god Olokun and teach him a lesson.

Conchobar (KAHN koh bahr), also called Conor, was the king of Ulster. He was a villain in many Irish myths.

Coyote (ky OH tee) was an evil god in myths of the Maidu and some other Native American people.

Crow (kroh) in Inuit myths was the wise bird who brought daylight to the Inuit people.

Cuchulain (koo KUHL ihn), also Cuchullain or Cuchulan, in Irish myths was Ireland's greatest warrior of all time. He was the son of Lug and Dechtire.

Culan (KOO luhn) in Irish myths was a blacksmith. His hound was killed by Setanta, who later became Cuchulain.

D

Davy Crockett (DAY vee KRAHK iht) was a real person. He is remembered as an American frontier hero who died in battle and also in legends as a great hunter and woodsman.

Dechtire (DEHK teer) in Irish myths was the sister of King Conchobar and mother of Cuchulain.

Deirdre (DAIR dray) in Irish myths was the daughter of Fedlimid. She refused to wed Conchobar. It was said that she would lead to Ireland's ruin.

Di Jun (dee joon) was god of the Eastern Sky in Chinese myths. He lived in a giant mulberry tree.

Di Zang Wang (dee zahng wahng) in Chinese myths was a Buddhist monk who was given that name when he became the lord of the underworld. His helper was Yan Wang, god of the dead.

Dionysus (dy uh NY suhs) was the god of wine in ancient Greek myths. He carried a staff wrapped in vines.

Dolapo was the wife of Kigbo in a Yoruba myth of Africa.

E

Eight Immortals (ihm MAWR tuhlz) in Chinese myths were eight ordinary human beings whose good deeds led them to truth and enlightenment. The Eight Immortals were godlike heroes. They had special powers to help people.

El Niño (ehl NEEN yoh) in Inca myths was the ruler of the wind, the weather, and the ocean and its creatures.

Emer (AYV ur) in Irish myths was the daughter of Forgal the Wily and wife of Cuchulain.

F

Fafnir (FAHV nihr) in Norse myths was a son of Hreidmar. He killed his father for his treasure, sent his brother Regin away, and turned himself into a dragon.

Frey (fray), also called Freyr, was the god of summer in Norse myths. His chariot was pulled by a huge wild boar.

Freya (FRAY uh) was the goddess of beauty and love in Norse myths. Her chariot was pulled by two large cats.

Frigga (FRIHG uh), also called Frigg, in Norse myths was the wife of Odin and mother of many gods. She was the most powerful goddess in Asgard.

Frog was an animal prince in an Alur myth of Africa. He and his brother, Lizard, competed for the right to inherit the throne of their father.

Fu Xi (foo shee) in a Chinese myth was a boy who, with his sister Nü Wa, freed the Thunder God and was rewarded. His name means Gourd Boy.

G

Gaunab was Death, who took on a human form in a Khoi myth of Africa. Tsui'goab fought with Gaunab to save his people.

Geb (gehb) in ancient Egypt was the Earth itself. All plants and trees grew from his back. He was the brother and husband of Nut and the father of the gods Osiris, Isis, Seth, and Nephthys.

Glooscap (glohs kap) was a brave and cunning god in the myths of Algonquian Native American people. He was a trickster who sometimes got tricked.

Guinevere (GWIHN uh vihr) in British and Welsh legends was King Arthur's queen, who was also loved by Sir Lancelot.

Gwydion (GWIHD ih uhn) in Welsh legends was the father of Llew and the nephew of the magician and ruler, Math.

H

Hades (HAY deez) in ancient Greece was the god of the dead. Hades was also called Pluto (PLOO toh). The Romans called him Dis.

Hairy Man was a frightening monster in African American folk tales.

Harpy (HAHRP ee) was one of the hideous winged women in Greek myths. The hero Jason and his Argonauts freed King Phineas from the harpies' power.

Hathor (HATH awr) was worshiped in the form of a cow in ancient Egypt, but she also appeared as an angry lioness. She was the daughter of Ra and the sister of Bastet and Sekhmet.

Heimdall (HAYM dahl) was the god in Norse myths who guarded the rainbow bridge joining Asgard, the home of the gods, to other worlds.

Hel (hehl), also called Hela, was the goddess of death in Norse myths. The lower half of her body was like a rotting corpse. Hel was Loki's daughter.

Helen (HEHL uhn), called Helen of Troy, was a real person in ancient Greece. According to legend, she was known as the most beautiful woman in the world. Her capture by Paris led to the Trojan War.

Heng E (huhng ay), sometimes called Chang E, was a woman in Chinese myths who became the moon goddess. She was the wife of Yi the Archer.

Hera (HEHR uh) in ancient Greece was the queen of heaven and the wife of Zeus. The Romans called her Juno.

Heracles (HEHR uh kleez) in ancient Greek myths was a hero of great strength. He was the son of Zeus. He had to complete twelve tremendous tasks in order to become one of the gods. The Romans called him Hercules.

Hermes (HUR meez) was the messenger of the gods in Greek myths. He wore winged sandals. The Romans called him Mercury.

Hoder (HOO dur) was Balder's twin brother in Norse myths. He was blind. It was said that after a mighty battle he and Balder would be born again.

Hoenir (HAY nihr), also called Honir, was a god in Norse myths. In some early myths, he is said to be Odin's brother.

Horus (HAWR uhs) in ancient Egypt was the son of Isis and Osiris. He was often shown with the head of a falcon. Horus fought Seth to rule Egypt.

Hreidmar (HRAYD mahr) was a dwarf king in Norse myths who held Odin for a huge pile of treasure. His sons were Otter, Fafnir, and Regin.

Hyrrokkin (HEER rahk kihn) in Norse myths was a terrifying female giant who rode an enormous wolf using poisonous snakes for reins.

I

Irin-Mage (eereen mah geh) in Tupinambá myths was the only person to be saved when the creator, Monan, destroyed the other humans. Irin-Mage became the ancestor of all people living today.

Isis (EYE sihs) in ancient Egypt was the goddess of fertility and a master of magic. She became the most powerful of all the gods and goddesses. She was the sister and wife of Osiris and mother of Horus.

J

Jade Emperor (jayd EHM puhr uhr) in Buddhist myths of China was the chief god in Heaven.

Jason (JAY suhn) was a hero in Greek myths. His ship was the Argo, and the men who sailed with him on his adventures were called the Argonauts.

Johnny Appleseed (AP uhl seed) was a real person, John Chapman. He is remembered in legends as the person who traveled across North America, planting apple orchards.

K

Kaboi (kah boy) was a very wise man in a Carajá myth. He helped his people find their way from their underground home to the surface of the earth.

Kewawkwuí (kay wow kwoo) were a group of powerful, frightening giants and magicians in the myths of Algonquian Native American people.

Kigbo (keeg boh) was a stubborn man in a Yoruba myth of Africa. His stubbornness got him into trouble with spirits.

Kodoyanpe (koh doh yahn pay) was a good god in the myths of the Maidu and some other Native American people. He was the brother of the evil god Coyote.

Kuang Zi Lian (kwahng dsee lee ehn) in a Taoist myth of China was a very rich, greedy farmer who was punished by one of the Eight Immortals.

Kui in Chinese myths was an ugly, brilliant scholar who became God of Examinations.

Kvasir (KVAH sihr) in Norse myths was the wisest of all the gods in Asgard.

L

Lancelot (lan suh laht) in British and Welsh legends was King Arthur's friend and greatest knight. He was secretly in love with Guinevere.

Lao Zi (low dzuh) was the man who founded the Chinese religion of Taoism. He wrote down the Taoist beliefs in a book, the *Tao Te Ching*.

Li Xuan (lee shwahn) was one of the Eight Immortals in ancient Chinese myths.

Light (lyt) was a child of Amma, the creator of the world, in a myth of the Dogon people of Africa.

Lizard (LIHZ urd) was an animal prince in an Alur myth of Africa. He was certain that he, and not his brother, Frog, would inherit the throne of their father.

Llew Llaw Gyffes (LE yoo HLA yoo GUHF ehs), also Lleu Law Gyffes, was a hero in Welsh myths who had many adventures. His mother was Arianrod and his father was Gwydion.

Loki (LOH kee) in Norse myths was a master trickster. His friends were Odin and Thor. Loki was half giant and half god, and could be funny and also cruel. He caused the death of Balder.

Lord of Heaven was the chief god in some ancient Chinese myths.

Lug (luk) in Irish myths was the Immortal High King of Ireland, Master of All Arts.

M

Maira-Monan (mah ee rah moh nahn) was the most powerful son of Irin-Mage in Tupinambá myths. He was destroyed by people who were afraid of his powers.

Manco Capac (mahn kih kah pahk) in Inca myths was the founder of the Inca people. He was one of four brothers and four sisters who led the Inca to their homeland.

Manitou (MAN ih toh) was the greatest and most powerful of all gods in Native American myths of the Iroquois people.

Math (mohth) in Welsh myths was a magician who ruled the Welsh kingdom of Gwynedd.

Michabo (mee chah boh) in the myths of Algonquian Native American people was the Great Hare, who taught people to hunt and brought them luck. He was a son of West Wind.

Monan (moh nahn) was the creator in Tupinambá myths.

Monkey (MUNG kee) is the hero of many Chinese stories. The most cunning of all monkeys, he became the king of monkeys and caused great troubles for the gods.

N

Nanook (na NOOK) was the white bear in myths of the Inuit people.

Naoise (NEE see) in Irish myths was Conchobar's nephew and the lover of Deirdre. He was the son of Usnech and brother of Ardan and Ainle.

Nekumonta (neh koo mohn tah) in Native American myths of the Iroquois people was a person whose goodness helped him save his people from a terrible sickness.

Nü Wa (nyuh wah) in a Chinese myth was a girl who, with her brother, Fu Xi, freed the Thunder God and was rewarded. Her name means Gourd Girl.

Nuada (NOO uh thuh) in Irish myths was King of the Tuatha Dé Danann, the rulers of all Ireland. He had a silver hand.

O

Odin (OH dihn), also called Woden, in Norse myths was the chief of all the gods and a brave warrior. He had only one eye. He was the husband of Frigga and father of many of the gods. His two advisers were the ravens Hugin and Munin.

Odysseus (oh DIHS ee uhs) was a Greek hero who fought in the Trojan War. The poet Homer wrote of his many adventures.

Oedipus (ED uh puhs) was a tragic hero in Greek myths. He unknowingly killed his own father and married his mother.

Olodumare (oh loh doo mah ray) was the supreme god in Yoruba myths of Africa.

Olokun (oh loh koon) was the god of water and giver of life in Yoruba myths of Africa. He challenged Olodumare for the right to rule.

Orpheus (AWR fee uhs) in Greek myths was famed for his music. He followed his wife, Euridice, to the kingdom of the dead to plead for her life.

Osiris (oh SY rihs) in ancient Egypt was the ruler of the dead in the kingdom of the West. He was the brother and husband of Isis and the father of Horus.

P

Pamola (pah moh lah) in the myths of Algonquian Native American people was an evil spirit of the night.

Pan Gu (pahn goo) in Chinese myths was the giant who was the first living being.

Pandora (pan DAWR uh) in ancient Greek myths was the first woman.

Paris (PAR ihs) was a real person, a hero from the city of Troy. He captured Helen, the queen of a Greek kingdom, and took her to Troy.

Paul Bunyan (pawl BUHN yuhn) was a tremendously strong giant lumberjack in North American myths.

Perseus (PUR see uhs) was a human hero in myths of ancient Greece. His most famous adventure was killing Medusa, a creature who turned anyone who looked at her to stone.

Poseidon (puh SY duhn) was the god of the sea in myths of ancient Greece. He carried a three-pronged spear called a trident to make storms and control the waves. The Romans called him Neptune.

Prometheus (pruh MEE thee uhs) was the cleverest of the gods in Greek myths. He was a friend to humankind.

Q

Queen Mother of the West was a goddess in Chinese myths.

R

Ra (rah), sometimes Re (ray), was the sun god of ancient Egypt. He was often shown with the head of a hawk. Re became the most important god. Other gods were sometimes combined with him and had Ra added to their names.

Ran (rahn) was the goddess of the sea in Norse myths. She pulled sailors from their boats in a large net and dragged them underwater.

Red Jacket in Chinese myths was an assistant to Wen Chang, the god of literature. His job was to help students who hadn't worked very hard.

S

Sekhmet (SEHK meht) in ancient Egypt was a blood-thirsty goddess with the head of a lioness. She was the daughter of Ra and the sister of Bastet and Hathor.

Setanta in Irish myths was Cuchulain's name before he killed the hound of Culan.

Seth (set), sometimes Set, in ancient Egypt was the god of chaos and confusion, who fought Horus to rule Egypt. He was the evil son of Geb and Nut.

Shanewis (shah nay wihs) in Native American myths of the Iroquois people was the wife of Nekumonta.

Shu (shoo) in ancient Egypt was the father of the sky goddess Nut. He held Nut above Geb, the Earth, to keep the two apart.

Sinchi Roca was the second emperor of the Inca. According to legend, he was the son of Ayar Manco (later known as Manco Capac) and his sister Mama Ocllo.

Skirnir (SKEER nihr) in Norse myths was a brave, faithful servant of the god Frey.

Sphinx (sfihngks) in Greek myths was a creature that was half lion and half woman, with eagle wings. It killed anyone who failed to answer its riddle.

T

Tefnut (TEHF noot) was the moon goddess in ancient Egypt. She was the sister and wife of Shu and the mother of Nut and Geb.

Theseus (THEE see uhs) was a human hero in myths of ancient Greece. He killed the Minotaur, a half-human, half-bull creature, and freed its victims.

Thor (thawr) was the god of thunder in Norse myths. He crossed the skies in a chariot pulled by goats and had a hammer, Mjollnir, and a belt, Meginjardir.

Thunder God (THUN dur gahd) in Chinese myths was the god of thunder and rain. He got his power from water and was powerless if he could not drink.

Tsui'goab (tsoo ee goh ahb) was the god of rain in myths of the Khoi people of Africa. He was a human who became a god after he fought to save his people.

Tupan (too pahn) was the spirit of thunder and lightning in Inca myths.

Tyr (tihr) was the god of war in Norse myths. He was the bravest god and was honorable and true, as well. He had just one hand.

U

Utgard-Loki (OOT gahrd LOH kee) in Norse myths was the clever, crafty giant king of Utgard. He once disguised himself as a giant called Skrymir to teach Thor a lesson.

W

Water God (WAW tur gahd) in Chinese myths was a god who sent rain and caused floods.

Wen Chang (wehn chuhng) in Chinese myths was the god of literature. His assistants were Kui and Red Jacket.

Wu (woo) was a lowly courtier in a Chinese myth who fell in love with a princess.

X

Xi He (shee heh) in Chinese myths was the goddess wife of Di Jun, the god of the eastern sky.

Xiwangmu (shee wahng moo) in Chinese myths was the owner of the Garden of Immortal Peaches.

Xuan Zang (shwahn dsahng), also called Tripitaka, was a real person, a Chinese Buddhist monk who traveled to India to gather copies of religious writings. Legends about him tell that Monkey was his traveling companion.

Y

Yan Wang (yahn wahng) was the god of the dead and judge of the first court of the Underworld in Chinese myths. He was helper to Di Zang Wang.

Yao (yow) was a virtuous emperor in Chinese myths. Because Yao lived simply and was a good leader, Yi the Archer was sent to help him.

Yi (yee) was an archer in Chinese myths who was sent by Di Jun to save the earth, in answer to Yao's prayers.

Z

Zeus (zoos) in ancient Greece was the king of gods and the god of thunder and lightning. The Romans called him Jupiter.

Zhao Shen Xiao (zhow shehn shi ow) in Chinese myths was a good magistrate, or official, who arrested the greedy merchant Kuang Zi Lian.

MYTHS AND LEGENDS GLOSSARY

This is a cumulative glossary of some important places and terms found in all eight volumes of the *World Book Myths and Legends* series.

A

Alfheim (AHLF hym) in Norse myth was the home of the light elves.

Asgard (AS gahrd) in Norse myths was the home of the warrior gods who were called the Aesir. It was connected to the earth by a rainbow bridge.

Augean (aw JEE uhn) stables were stables that the Greek hero Heracles had to clean as one of his twelve labors. He made the waters of two rivers flow through the stables and wash away the filth.

Avalon (AV uh lahn) in British legends was the island where King Arthur was carried after he died in battle. The legend says he will rise again to lead Britain.

B

Bard (bahrd) was a Celtic poet and singer in ancient times. A bard entertained people by making up and singing poems about brave deeds.

Battle of the Alamo (AL uh moh) was a battle between Texas settlers and Mexican forces when Texas was fighting for independence from Mexico. It took place at the Alamo, a fort in San Antonio, in 1836.

Bifrost (BEE fruhst) in Norse myths was a rainbow bridge that connected Asgard with the world of people.

Black Land in ancient Egypt was the area of fertile soil around the banks of the River Nile. Most people lived there.

Brer Rabbit (brair RAB iht) myths are African American stories about a rabbit who played tricks on his friends. The stories grew out of animal myths from Africa.

C

Canoe Mountain in a Maidu myth of North America was the mountain on which the evil Coyote took refuge from a flood sent to drown him.

Changeling (CHAYNG lihng) in Celtic myths was a fairy child who had been swapped with a human baby at birth. Changelings were usually lazy and clumsy.

Confucianism (kuhn FYOO shuhn IHZ uhm) is a Chinese way of life and religion. It is based on the teachings of Confucius, also known as Kong Fu Zi, and is more than 2,000 years old.

Creation myths (kree AY shuhn mihths) are myths that tell how the world began.

D

Dwarfs (dwawrfs) in Norse myths were small people of great power. They were skilled at making tools and weapons.

F

Fairies (FAIR eez) in Celtic myths were called the Little People. They are especially common in Irish legends, where they are called leprechauns.

Fomors (FOH wawrz) in Irish myths were hideous giants who invaded Ireland and were fought by Lug.

G

Giants (JY uhnts) in Norse myths were huge people who had great strength and great powers. They often struggled with the warrior gods of Asgard.

Gnome (nohm) was a small, odd-looking person in the myths of many civilizations. In Inca myths, for example, gnomes were tiny people with very big beards.

Golden Apples of the Hesperides (heh SPEHR uh deez) were apples of gold in a garden that only the Greek gods could enter. They were collected by the hero Heracles as one of his twelve labors.

Golden fleece was the fleece of a ram that the Greek hero Jason won after many adventures with his ship, Argo, and his companion sailors, the Argonauts.

Green Knoll (nohl) was the home of the Little People, or fairies, in Irish and Scottish myths.

J

Jotunheim (YUR toon hym) in Norse myths was the land of the giants.

L

Lion men in myths of Africa were humans who can turn themselves into lions.

Little People in Celtic legends and folk tales are fairies. They are often fine sword makers and blacksmiths.

M

Machu Picchu (MAH choo PEE choo) is the ruins of an ancient city built by the Inca in the Andes Mountains of Peru.

Medecolin (may day coh leen) were a tribe of evil sorcerers in the myths of Algonquian Native American people.

Medicine (MEHD uh sihn) **man** is a wise man or shaman who has special powers. Medicine men also appear as beings with special powers in myths of Africa and North and South America. Also see **Shaman.**

Midgard (MIHD gahrd) in Norse myths was the world of people.

Muspell (MOOS pehl) in Norse myths was part of the Underworld. It was a place of fire.

N

Nidavellir in Norse myths was the land of the dwarfs.

Niflheim in Norse myths was part of the Underworld. It included Hel, the kingdom of the dead.

Nirvana (nur VAH nuh) in the religion of Buddhism is a state of happiness that people find when they have freed themselves from wanting things. People who reach Nirvana no longer have to be reborn.

O

Oracle (AWRR uh kuhl) in ancient Greece was a sacred place served by people who could foretell the future. Greeks journeyed there to ask questions about their fortunes. Also see **Soothsayer.**

P

Pacariqtambo (pahk kah ree TAHM boh) in Inca myths was a place of three caves from which the first people stepped out into the world. It is also called Paccari Tampu.

Poppykettle was a clay kettle made for brewing poppy-seed tea. In an Inca myth, a poppykettle was used for a boat.

Prophecy (PRAH feh see) is a prediction made by someone who foretells the future.

R

Ragnarok (RAHG nah ruhk) in Norse myths was the final battle of good and evil, in which the giants would fight against the gods of Asgard.

S

Sahara (sah HAH rah) is a vast desert that covers much of northern Africa.

Seriema was a bird in a Carajá myth of South America whose call led the first people to try to find their way from underground to the surface of the earth.

Shaman (SHAH muhn) can be a real person, a medicine man or wise person who knows the secrets of nature. Shamans also appear as beings with special powers in some myths of North and South America. Also see **Medicine man.**

Soothsayer (sooth SAY ur) in ancient Greece was someone who could see into the future. Also see **Oracle.**

Svartalfheim (SVAHRT uhl hym) in Norse myths was the home of the dark elves.

T

Tar Baby was a sticky doll made of tar used to trap Brer Rabbit, a tricky rabbit in African American folk tales.

Tara (TAH rah) in Irish myths was the high seat, or ruling place, of the Irish kings.

Trickster (TRIHK stur) **animals** are clever ones that appear in many myths of North America, South America, and Africa.

Trojan horse. See **Wooden horse of Troy.**

Tuatha dÈ Danann (THOO uh huh day DUH nuhn) were the people of the goddess Danu. Later they were known as gods of Ireland themselves.

V

Vanaheim (VAH nah hym) in Norse myths was the home of the fertility gods.

W

Wadjet eye was a symbol used by the people of ancient Egypt. It stood for the eye of the gods Ra and Horus and was supposed to bring luck.

Wheel of Transmigration (tranz my GRAY shuhn) in the religion of Buddhism is the wheel people's souls reach after they die. From there they are sent back to earth to be born into a higher or lower life.

Wooden horse of Troy was a giant wooden horse built by the Greeks during the Trojan War. The Greeks hid soldiers in the horse's belly and left the horse for the Trojans to find.

Y

Yang (yang) is the male quality of light, sun, heat, and dryness in Chinese beliefs. Yang struggles with Yin for control of things.

Yatkot was a magical tree in an African myth of the Alur people.

Yggdrasil (IHG drah sihl) in Norse myths was a mighty tree that held all three worlds together and reached up into the stars.

Yin (yihn) is the female quality of shadow, moon, cold, and water in Chinese beliefs. Yin struggles with Yang for control of things.

CUMULATIVE INDEX

This is an alphabetical list of important topics covered in all eight volumes of the **World Book Myths and Legends** series. Next to each entry is at least one pair of numbers separated by a slash mark (/). For example, the entry for Argentina is "**Argentina 8/4**". The first number tells you what volume to look in for information. The second number tells you what page you should turn to in that volume. Sometimes a topic appears in more than one place. When it does, additional volume and page numbers are given. Here's a reminder of the volume numbers and titles: 1, *African Myths and Legends*; 2, *Ancient Egyptian Myths and Legends*; 3, *Ancient Greek Myths and Legends*; 4, *Celtic Myths and Legends*; 5, *Chinese Myths and Legends*; 6, *Norse Myths and Legends*; 7, *North American Myths and Legends*; 8, *South American Myths and Legends*.

For information on other World Book products, visit our Web site at www.worldbook.com or call 1-800-WORLDBK (967-5325).

For information on sales to schools and libraries, call 1-800-975-3250.

Cover background illustration by Paul Perreault

World Book, Inc.
233 North Michigan Avenue
Chicago, IL 60601

Pages 1–47: format and illustrations, ©1997 Belitha Press; text, ©1997 Philip Ardagh

Printed in the United States of America
1 2 3 4 5 6 7 8 9 10 10 09 08 07 06 05 04 03 02 01

ISBN(set): 0-7166-2613-6

African Myths and Legends
ISBN: 0-7166-2605-5
LC: 2001026492

Ancient Egyptian Myths and Legends
ISBN: 0-7166-2606-3
LC: 2001026501

Ancient Greek Myths and Legends
ISBN: 0-7166-2607-1
LC: 2001035959

Celtic Myths and Legends
ISBN: 0-7166-2608-X
LC: 20011026496

Chinese Myths and Legends
ISBN: 0-7166-2609-8
LC: 2001026489

Norse Myths and Legends
ISBN: 0-7166-2610-1
LC: 2001026488

North American Myths and Legends
ISBN: 0-7166-2611-X
LC: 2001026490

South American Myths and Legends
ISBN: 0-7166-2612-8
LC: 2001026491